1001 Blues Licks

by Toby Wine

ISBN 978-1-57560-536-4

Visit our website at www.cherrylane.com

Introduction

The melodies, rhythms, forms, and inflections of the blues so completely permeate every style of contemporary music that they're often taken for granted. You'll find blues "licks" in television commercials and film scores, under the sheen of a glossy pop tune, at the heart of heavy metal, in modern classical music and opera, on a jazz bandstand, or at the Grand Ole Opry. Nearly all of today's music is influenced or informed in some way—consciously or not—by the blues. As such, the blues is worthy and deserving of any serious musician's attention and study. What began as a forlorn but defiant testimony to the tribulations of the African slaves, their ancestors, and their generations to come evolved into a virtuoso art form in its own right and spawned a sound that changed the world.

Whether you're a beginner or an experienced blues player, a rabid fan or a curious newcomer, *1001 Blues Licks* is sure to offer a wealth of new ideas to enrich your music. This book contains a massive collection of licks, riffs, and other melodic material inspired by the master blues musicians of the past and present and their distinctive styles. Even the most diehard devotee is bound to find something new and challenging here, while fresh converts will find this a stepping stone to a richer, blues-inflected style of their own.

About the Author

A freelance guitarist, composer, arranger, and teacher, Toby Wine lives in New York City and is a graduate of the Manhattan School of Music. Toby has performed with Philip Harper, Bob Mover, Joe Shepley, Ari Ambrose, Michael and Carolyn Leonhart, and John Ryerson, among others. His arrangements can be heard on Philip Harper's Muse CDs *Soulful Sin* and *The Thirteenth Moon*, and his composition "Venus" can be heard on CDs by Ari Ambrose (Steeplechase) and Ian Hendrickson Smith (Kpasta). Toby occasionally leads his own trio and septet, does studio recordings, and has worked as an orchestrator and score preparer for avant-garde innovator Ornette Coleman. In addition to work as an arranger and musical director for a variety of vocalists, Toby is also the music librarian for the Carnegie Hall Jazz Band and is a freelance writer (including the Cherry Lane publications *Steely Dan: Legendary Licks*, *The Art of Texas Blues Guitar*, and others) and editor. His studies have included work with Walter Davis, Jr., Bob Mover, Ken Wessel, Bern Nix, Ed Green, and Manny Albam.

Toby Wine

Acknowledgments

Many thanks to the following folks for their help, influence, patience, and attention: Ari, Bibi, Bob, Bloom, David, Enid, Grits, Indiana Dave, Jack S. and Jack W., Arthur and Joe C., Kenny, Manny, Mark, Mover, Plum, Sammy, Thaddeus, and the ever-helpful Mark Phillips at Cherry Lane.

And especially, my parents, Rosemary and Jerry.

Table of Contents

Notes on the Licks

Consider this book a compendium, encyclopedia, or reference work. It is not intended to be read or played from cover to cover. Instead, find your own uses for the material—whether it's picking out a few licks here and there to add to your repertoire, studying one of the regional styles examined in the pages that follow, or any other purpose that strikes you. The blues has been, historically, a guitar-dominated style, but instrumentalists of all kinds have made important contributions, and their work hasn't been neglected here. Vocalists, harpists, saxophonists, trumpeters, pianists, and others have played a large part in the development and popularity of the music. Whatever your instrument, in the pages that follow you'll find material inspired by a variety of styles, offering fresh challenges and new perspectives to enrich your own playing.

There was much deliberation before this project began regarding the organization of the many licks involved. After a number of about-faces, we decided to group them by regional style rather than by tempo, feel, or a variety of other classifications. While this system is admittedly not perfect, it seems to offer less difficulty and suggests more variety than other methods. Defining a lick as "slow blues" or "shuffle feel" limits a lick's potential instead of expanding on it, and while a Delta blues lick may closely resemble a Texas or Memphis lick, it was, after all, inspired by one of the great Delta bluesmen. Licks are handed down from generation to generation, criss-crossing the globe on flying fingers and in attentive ears, almost defying categorization by definition. Regardless, each and every lick herein was inspired by or closely paraphrases the music of actual performers of various regional styles. A tremendous amount of research and listening was involved, ensuring the material's quality and authenticity.

Nothing in this book is rigid or inflexible. While each set of 100 regional licks is divided into three sections—one each for the first, second, and third four-measure groupings within a conventional 12-bar blues form (the simplest and most familiar palette for the licks)—try playing them in different places in the blues and over a variety of chords and forms. By the way, there are some licks that are longer than four measures—they "spill over" into the next section within the 12-bar blues framework. Each lick is presented in the key of C for uniformity and simplicity, but you should feel free to learn how to play your favorites in all keys to have them at your disposal in a wide range of musical settings. No tempo or feel descriptors have been used, and while a lick may suggest one through its rhythms or density, you'll find many have a surprising versatility and can adapt to different rhythmic environments. Obviously, licks made up of predominately long rhythmic values (whole notes and half notes) work best at faster tempos, while those crammed with 16th and 32nd notes usually work better at slower speeds where they sound less frantic. You may also want to move the licks to higher or lower registers, or take a fragment out of the context of the whole. By all means, do. Each lick is a complete phrase unto itself, but can be re-used, re-imagined, and re-interpreted any way you like.

This is the blues, an expression of individuality and soul. Please seek out the music, words, and performances of those masters here and gone, and let their work, like this book, guide you towards the creation of your own unique musical voice.

Delta Blues Licks

Inspired by men like Son House, Robert Johnson, Skip James, Mississippi John Hurt, and the young Muddy Waters, Delta blues were often played in slow, "swing" type feels, much like early jazz, or uptempo "boogie" rhythms. Many of these classifications came later on and were not used by the musicians at the time of the music's creation. Delta blues was not a virtuoso instrumental style but laid the foundation for the music to come, is steeped in emotion, and bears testimony to the hardships of rural life in the early part of the 20th century.

Country Blues Licks

These licks employ, for the most part, similar rhythmic feels to the Delta material and were in fact inspired by some of the same musicians. Country blues proliferated in the American south in the 1920s and 1930s and some of its greatest practitioners included Big Bill Broonzy, Leadbelly, "Blind" Willie McTell, Josh White, and the great Lonnie Johnson. Country blues does not refer to the Southern rock pioneered by bands like Lynyrd Skynyrd, Alabama, and Molly Hatchet, although if you listen closely, you can probably detect an influence of one on the other.

Chicago Blues Licks

These are some of our most beloved and familiar licks, inspired by masters like Muddy Waters, B.B. King, Junior Wells, Buddy Guy, Otis Spann, Elmore James, and Jimmy Reed, among many others. You can find all manners of rhythmic feels in Chicago blues, but harp-blown, hard driving shuffles, and slow, smoldering 12/8 grooves predominate.

Texas Blues Licks

The Texas style is very similar to that of Chicago, and it even shares more than a few of its leading lights (blues musicians being notoriously nomadic). The Texas style is marked by hard-swinging rhythm sections, jazz-influenced horns, and a swaggering, bravado presence. T-Bone Walker, Albert Collins, Johnny Winter, Stevie Ray Vaughan, Freddie King, and Johnny Copeland all influenced the licks you'll find here.

Memphis Blues Licks

Joe Hill Louis, James Cotton, Memphis Slim, Pinetop Perkins, Little Junior's Blue Flames, and the rest of the Sun Records roster of fine blues acts inspired the licks in this section. They represent a cross-section of country and urban blues from the early 1950s that would soon be influencing a new style: the earliest incarnations of rock 'n' roll.

Jump Blues Licks

If ever a style truly bridged the gap between blues, jazz, and rock 'n' roll, jump was it. Upbeat, fun, and great for dancing, jump blues was dominated by performers like Louis Jordan, Sam Price, Little Richard, Tarheel Slim, and Professor Longhair, who rode swing, relentless riffs, strong soloists, and zany lyrics to immense popularity in the years between the end of World War II and the onset of the rock 'n' roll craze.

Jazz Blues Licks

Musicians like Charlie Parker, Charlie Christian, Duke Ellington, Wes Montgomery, John Coltrane, and Herbie Hancock brought new levels of sophistication to the blues, and the licks they inspired here reflect that. You'll find varied chord progressions, chromaticism, harmonic substitutions, and elegant turns of phrase in this section as well. Play these licks with a swing feel, and if you're new to jazz, get ready for some fresh and unusual sounds and ideas.

Rock and Funk Blues Licks

Rock 'n' roll and blues have gone hand-in-hand since rock's inception, with everyone from Chuck Berry to Jimi Hendrix, Eric Clapton, and Jimmy Page inspiring our material. These are some of the fastest, most difficult licks of the book, so take your time with them and patiently work them up to speed. A variety of feels are represented here as well, including traditional "Johnny B. Goode"–style rock 'n' roll, heavy "Voodoo Chile"–inspired half-time feels, straight eighth note grooves (think "Sunshine of Your Love"), and over-driven shuffles.

Louisiana Blues Licks

The people of New Orleans and Louisiana as a whole are staunch individualists and a friendly, inclusive bunch as well. The Louisiana blues reflects this, with a variety of influences, from jazz, Cajun, Creole, zydeco, rock, and country all chiming in. The licks here, inspired by a diverse group that includes Earl King and Roomful of Blues, Dr. John, Bobby Charles, Chubby Carrier, Rudi Richard, Henry Gray, and C.J. Chenier, come in all shapes and sizes, but are often played over a 3:2 *clave* (a two-measure phrase consisting of a dotted quarter note, a second dotted quarter, and an undotted quarter in the first measure, and a quarter note rest, two quarter notes, and another quarter note rest in the second measure). This type of groove and its variants are often referred to as a "second-line" feel.

Minor Blues Licks

Here's a brief glimpse into how the blues is applied to minor progressions and some of the chord variations encountered in this form. The minor blues are very common in jazz but less so in other styles, although they are played. Many of the other licks can be adaptable to minor settings as well.

Blues Waltz Licks

The blues in 3/4 is much more common in jazz than in other styles, but it does crop up, especially in slow, country ballads that may be blues at its very gentlest. This short section suggests just a few ways in which the blues and blues vocabulary can be used in waltz time.

Delta Blues Licks—First Four Measures

6

19

20

21

22

23

24

25

26

27

28

29

30

31

32

33

34

Delta Blues Licks—Second Four Measures

35

36

37

38

39

40

41

42

43

44

45

46

47

48

49

50

60

61

62

63

64

65

66

67

Delta Blues Licks—Final Four Measures

68

69

70

71

72

73

74

75

76

77

78

79

80

81

82

83

84

85

86

87

88

89

90

91

92

93

94

95

96

97

98

99

100

Country Blues Licks—First Four Measures

101

102

103

104

105

106

107

108

109

110

111

112

113

114

115

116

117

118

119

120

121

122

123

124

125

126

127

128

129

130

131

132

133

134

Country Blues Licks—Second Four Measures

135

136

137

138

139

140

141

142

143

144

145

146

147

148

149

150

151

152

153

154

155

Country Blues Licks—Final Four Measures

167

168

169

170

171

172

173

174

175

176

177

178

179

180

181

182

183

184

185

186

187

188

189

190

191

192

193

194

195

196

197

198

199

200

Chicago Blues Licks—First Four Measures

201

202

203

204

205

206

207

208

209

210

211

212

213

214

215

216

217

218

219

220

221

222

223

224

225

226

227

228

229

230

231

232

233

234

Chicago Blues Licks—Second Four Measures

235

236

237

238

239

240

241

242

243

244

245

246

247

248

249

250

251

252

253

254

255

256

257

258

Chicago Blues Licks—Final Four Measures

268

269

270

271

272

273

274

275

276

277

278

279

280

281

282

283

284

285

286

287

288

289

290

291

292

293

294

295

296

297

298

299

300

Texas Blues Licks—First Four Measures

301

302

303

304

305

306

307

308

309

310

311

312

313

314

315

316

317

318

319

320

321

322

323

324

325

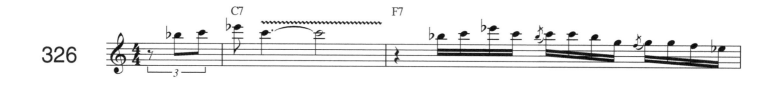

326

327

328

329

330

331

332

333

334

Texas Blues Licks—Second Four Measures

335

336

337

338

339

340

341

342

343

344

345

346

347

348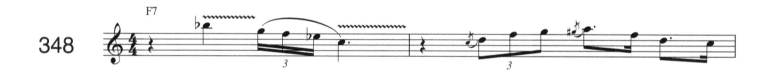

349

350

351

352

353

354

355

356

357

358

359

360

361

362

363

364

365

366

367

Texas Blues Licks—Final Four Measures

368

369

370

371

372

373

374

375

376

377

378

379

380

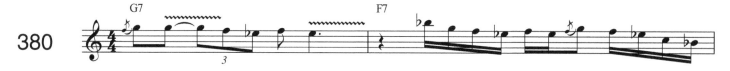

381

382

383

384

385

386

387

388

389

390

391

Memphis Blues Licks—First Four Measures

401

402

403

404

405

406

407

408

409

410

411

412
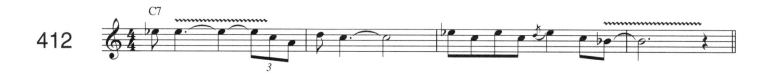

413

414

415

416

417

418

419

420

421

422

423

424

425

426

427

428

429

430

431

432

433

434

Memphis Blues Licks—Second Four Measures

435

436

437

438

439

440

441

442

443

444

445

446

447

448

449

450

451

461

462

463

464

465

466

467

Memphis Blues Licks—Final Four Measures

468

469

470

471

472

473

474

475

476

477

478

479

480

481

482

483

484

485

486

487

488

489

490

491

492

493

494

495

496

497

498

499

500

Jump Blues Licks—First Four Measures

501

502

503

504

505

506

507

508

509

519

520

521

522

523

524

525

526

527

528

529

530

531

532

533

534

Jump Blues Licks—Second Four Measures

535

536

537

538

539

540

541

542

543

544

545

546

547

548

549

550

551

552

553

554

555

556

557

558

559

560

561

562

563

564

565

566

567

Jump Blues Licks—Final Four Measures

578

579

580

581

582

583

584

585

586

587

588

589

590

591

592

593

594

595

596

597

598

599

600

Jazz Blues Licks—First Four Measures

601

602

603

604

605

606

607

608

609

610

611

612

613

614

615

616

617

618

619

620

621

622

623

624

625

626

627

628

629

630

631

632

633

Jazz Blues Licks—Second Four Measures

634

635

636

637

638

639

640

641

642

643

644

645

646

647

648

649

650

651

652

653

654

655

656

657

658

659

660

661

662

663

664

665

666

Jazz Blues Licks—Final Four Measures

667

668

669

670

671

672

673

674

675

676

677

678

679

680

681

682

683

684

685

686

687

688

689

690

691

692

693

694

695

696

697

698

699

700

Rock and Funk Blues Licks—First Four Measures

701

702

703

704

705

706

707

708

709

710

711

712

713

714

715

716

717

718

719

720

721

722

723

724

725

726

727

728

729

730

731

732

733

734

Rock and Funk Blues Licks—Second Four Measures

735

736

737

738

739

740

741

742

743

744

745

746

747

748

749

750

751

752

753

754

755

756

757

758

759

760

761

762

763

764

765

766

767

Rock and Funk Blues Licks—Final Four Measures

768

769

770

771

772

773

774

775

776

777

778

779

780

781

782

783

784

785

786

787

788

789

790

791

792

793

794

795

796

797

798

799

800

Louisiana Blues Licks—First Four Measures

801

802

803

804

805

806

807

808

809

810

811

812

813

814

815

816

817

818

819

820

821

822

823

824

825

826

827

828

829

830

831

832

833

834

Louisiana Blues Licks—Second Four Measures

835

836

837

838

839

840

841

842

843

844

845

846

847

848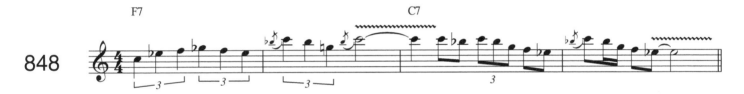

849

850

851

852

853

854

855

856

857

858

859

860

861

862

863

864

865

866

867

Louisiana Blues Licks—Final Four Measures

868

869

870

871

872

873

874

875

876

877

878

879

880

881

882

883

884

885

886

887

888

889

890

891

892

893

894

895

896

897

898

899

900

Minor Blues Licks—First Four Measures

901

902

903

904

905

906

907

908

909

910

911

912

913

914

915

916

917

Minor Blues Licks—Second Four Measures

918

919

920

921

922

923

924

925

926

927

928

929

930

931

932

933

Minor Blues Licks—Final Four Measures

934

935

936

937

938

939

940

941

942

943

944

945

946

947

948

949

950

Blues Waltz Licks—First Four Measures

951

952

953

954

955

956

957

958

959

960

961

962

963

964

965

966

967

Blues Waltz Licks—Second Four Measures

968

969

970

971

972

973

974

975

976

977

978

979

980

981

982

983

984

Blues Waltz Licks—Final Four Measures

994

995

996

997

998

999
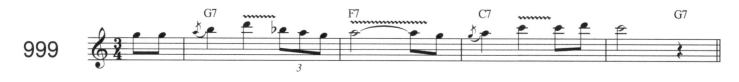

1000

1001